HISTORY'S MOST INFLUENTIAL
MUSICIANS

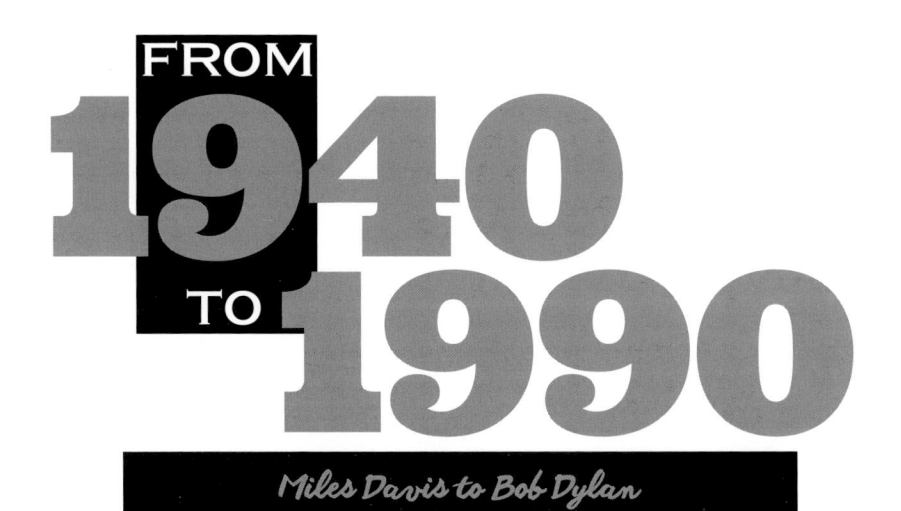

FROM 1940 TO 1990

Miles Davis to Bob Dylan

EDITED BY GINI GORLINSKI

Britannica®
Educational Publishing

IN ASSOCIATION WITH

ROSEN
EDUCATIONAL SERVICES

Published in 2024 by Britannica Educational Publishing
(a trademark of Encyclopædia Britannica, Inc.)
in association with Rosen Educational Services, LLC
2544 Clinton Street, Buffalo, NY 14224.

Copyright © 2024 Encyclopædia Britannica, Inc. Britannica, Encyclopædia Britannica, and the Thistle logo are registered trademarks of Encyclopædia Britannica, Inc. All rights reserved.

Rosen Educational Services materials copyright © 2024 Rosen Educational Services, LLC. All rights reserved.

Distributed exclusively by Rosen Educational Services.
For a listing of additional Britannica Educational Publishing titles, call toll free (800) 237-9932.

First Edition

Britannica Educational Publishing
Michael I. Levy: Executive Editor
Marilyn L. Barton: Senior Coordinator, Production Control
Steven Bosco: Director, Editorial Technologies
Lisa S. Braucher: Senior Producer and Data Editor
Yvette Charboneau: Senior Copy Editor
Kathy Nakamura: Manager, Media Acquisition
Gini Gorlinski, Associate Editor, Music and Dance
Diana Solomon, Copy Editor

Editor: Greg Roza
Book design: Michael Flynn

Photo credits: Cover https://commons.wikimedia.org/wiki/File:Televisie-optreden_van_The_Beatles_in_Treslong_te_Hillegom_vlnr._Paul_McCartney,_Bestanddeelnr_916-5099.jpg; p. 15; p. 23 https://commons.wikimedia.org/wiki/File:Elvis_Presley_Jailhouse_Rock.jpg; p. 33 https://commons.wikimedia.org/wiki/File:Mick_Jagger_(1976).jpg; p. 43 https://commons.wikimedia.org/wiki/File:Beatles_with_Ed_Sullivan.jpg; p. 48 https://commons.wikimedia.org/wiki/File:Joan_Baez_Bob_Dylan.jpg; p. 59 https://commons.wikimedia.org/wiki/File:Bob_Dylan_June_23_1978.jpg.

Cataloging-in-Publication Data

Names: Gorlinski, Gini.
Title: Influential musicians: from 1940 to 1990 — Miles Davis to Bob Dylan / Gini Gorlinski.
Description: New York : Britannica Educational Publishing, in Association with Rosen Educational Services. 2024. | Series: History's most influential musicians | Includes glossary and index.
Identifiers: ISBN 9781499475036 (library bound) | ISBN 9781499475029 (pbk) | ISBN 9781499475043 (ebook)
Subjects: LCSH: Musicians--Biography--Juvenile literature. | Musicians--Juvenile literature.
Classification: LCC ML3929.G67 2024 | DDC 780.92'2 B--dc23

Manufactured in the United States of America

CPSIA Compliance Information: Batch #CSBRIT24. For further information contact Rosen Publishing at 1-800-237-9932.

Find us on

CONTENTS

Introduction 4
Miles Davis 6
Chuck Berry 9
Antonio Carlos Jobim 12
Ray Charles 14
Patsy Cline 16
James Brown 18
Elvis Presley 21
Luciano Pavarotti 26
Buddy Holly 28
The Rolling Stones 30
Philip Glass 36
Smokey Robinson and the Miracles . . 37
Parliament-Funkadelic 39
The Beatles 41
Joan Baez 47
Plácido Domingo 49
The Beach Boys 50
Bob Dylan 54
Glossary 62
For More Information 63
Index 64

Introduction

"Look, man, all I am is a trumpet player. I can only do one thing—play my horn . . . I ain't no entertainer and I ain't trying to be one. I am one thing, a musician." —Miles Davis

What is influence? Is it the power that one individual holds to change the world? Is it prestige—the glimmering reputation earned by those who have achieved excellence or superiority? Or is it that sense of immortality bestowed on certain people who, through their lives, their actions, and their accomplishments, have climbed pedestals so high and prominent that they are virtually guaranteed a place in the books of history?

Influence can mean so many things and is therefore hard to define. But this much is clear: in a book such as this, where the subject is influential musicians, an exact definition hardly matters. Such artists may exert themselves in all kinds of ways—through their compositions, lyrics, performances, or even through "extracurricular" activities such as raising funds for charitable causes and organizations.

Simply put, great music is more than just music. It makes us think; it makes us feel. And over 20, 30, even hundreds of years, it continues to make us listen. In the world of music, that is influence. There are, of course, those musicians who, as childhood prodigies, seem not to have needed outside influence to exert their own. Frédéric Chopin began playing piano at age seven, gave his first concert a year later, and at age eleven performed for the Russian tsar Alexander I. Mozart, whose life was all too short although with an extraordinary influence, was composing from the age of five.

Introduction

As for the music experience and its delivery, today is quite different than just a few short years ago. Records, cassette tapes, and CDs are all but gone. In the 21st century, we have ear buds and smartphones, we stream music online from sites such as Spotify, Amazon Music, Apple Music, and Pandora. Music today is digital. It is fast, at our fingertips, and often it is free. The current profile will undoubtedly change in the future—it always does.

But then again, you can also be sure that much will be the same. We will always listen to music through whatever device we choose. Music will always be a part of our lives, ringing through our ears even when it is silent and nothing but a memory. People will always sing as they shower, turn it up as they drive, and "tune out" as they try to ignore everything else in their lives. That is music, and that is the influence it has on us.

Those musicians featured in this book span hundreds of years, countless musical genres, and immeasurable distances in style, technique, and purpose. Nevertheless, they have all been, and continue to be, influential. Some are influential because they brought a unique approach to their art that others later followed. Others were leaders of an influential movement in their field—a movement that led future musicians to improvise, change, and ultimately re-create music itself. And still others, through their work, brought about social reform and societal change that has forever shaped the landscape in which we now live.

For these influential people, music was and is life. Tchaikovsky, Stravinsky, Rachmaninoff. Springsteen, Sinatra, Madonna. They devoted their careers to the art, spending countless hours writing, creating, and fine-tuning. They have performed for great crowds, spoken on their beliefs, stood up for just causes, and above all, brought pleasure to the people who have listened. In doing so, each has left a mark, a stamp of influence, on the world.

MILES DAVIS

(b. May 26, 1926, Alton, Ill., U.S.—d. Sept. 28, 1991, Santa Monica, Calif.)

American jazz musician Miles Dewey Davis III—or simply, Miles Davis—was a great trumpeter who as a bandleader and composer was one of the major influences on the art from the late 1940s.

STARTING OUT

Davis grew up in East St. Louis, Ill., where his father was a prosperous dental surgeon. He began studying trumpet in his early teens; fortuitously, in light of his later stylistic development, his first teacher advised him to play without vibrato. Davis played with jazz bands in the St. Louis area before moving to New York City in 1944 to study at the Institute of Musical Art (now the Juilliard School)—although he skipped many classes and instead was schooled through jam sessions with masters such as Dizzy Gillespie and Charlie Parker. Davis and Parker recorded together often during the years 1945–48.

Davis's early playing was sometimes tentative and not always fully in tune, but his unique, intimate tone and his fertile musical imagination outweighed his technical shortcomings. By the early 1950s Davis had turned his limitations into considerable assets. Davis explored the trumpet's middle register, experimenting with harmonies and rhythms and varying the phrasing of his improvisations. With the occasional exception of multinote flurries, his melodic style was direct and unornamented.

Cool Jazz and Modal Jazz

In the summer of 1948, Davis formed a nonet that included the renowned jazz artists Gerry Mulligan, J.J. Johnson, Kenny Clarke, and Lee Konitz, as well as players on French horn and tuba, instruments rarely heard in a jazz context. Mulligan, Gil Evans, and pianist John Lewis did most of the band's arrangements, which juxtaposed the flexible, improvisatory nature of bebop with a thickly textured orchestral sound. The group was short-lived but during its brief history recorded a dozen tracks that were originally released as singles (1949–50). These recordings changed the course of modern jazz and paved the way for the West Coast styles of the 1950s. The tracks were later collected in the album *Birth of the Cool* (1957).

During the early 1950s Davis recorded albums that rank among his best. In 1954, having overcome drug addiction, Davis embarked on a two-decade period during which he was considered the most innovative musician in jazz. He formed classic small groups in the 1950s that featured saxophone legends John Coltrane and Cannonball Adderley, pianists Red Garland and Bill Evans, bassist Paul Chambers, and drummers "Philly" Joe Jones and Jimmy Cobb. Davis's albums recorded during this era, including *'Round About Midnight* (1956), *Steamin'* (1956), and *Milestones* (1958), among others, affected the work of numerous other artists. He capped this period of his career with *Kind of Blue* (1959), perhaps the most celebrated album in the history of jazz. A mellow, relaxed collection, the album includes the finest recorded examples of modal jazz, a style in which improvisations are based upon sparse chords and nonstandard scales rather than on complex, frequently changing chords.

Released concurrently with the small-group recordings, Davis's albums with pieces arranged and conducted by Gil Evans—*Miles Ahead* (1957), *Porgy and Bess* (1958), and *Sketches of Spain* (1960)—were also monuments of the genre. The Davis-Evans collaborations were marked by complex arrangements, a near-equal emphasis on orchestra and soloist, and some of Davis's most soulful and emotionally powerful playing. Davis and Evans occasionally collaborated in later years, but never again so memorably as on these three masterful albums.

Free Jazz and Fusion

The early 1960s were transitional, less-innovative years for Davis. He began forming another soon-to-be-classic small group in late 1962 with bassist Ron Carter, pianist Herbie Hancock, and teenage drummer Tony Williams; tenor saxophonist Wayne Shorter joined the lineup in 1964. Davis's new quintet was characterized by a light, free sound and a repertoire that extended from the blues to avant-garde and free jazz. Compared with the innovations of other modern jazz groups of the 1960s, the Davis quintet's experimentations in polyrhythm and polytonality were more subtle but equally daring. *Live at the Plugged Nickel* (1965), *E.S.P.* (1965), *Miles Smiles* (1966), and *Nefertiti* (1967) were among the quintet's timeless, influential recordings. About the time of *Miles in the Sky* and *Filles de Kilimanjaro* (both 1968), Davis began experimenting with electronic instruments. With other musicians, including keyboardists Chick Corea and Joe Zawinul and guitarist John McLaughlin, Davis cut *In a Silent Way* (1969), regarded as the seminal album of the jazz fusion movement. It was considered by purists to be Davis's last true jazz album.

Davis won new fans and alienated old ones with the release of *Bitches Brew* (1969), an album on which he fully embraced the rhythms, electronic instrumentation, and studio effects of rock music. A cacophonous kaleidoscope of layered sounds, rhythms, and textures, the album's influence was heard in such 1970s fusion groups as Weather Report and Chick Corea's Return to Forever. Davis continued in this style for a few years, with the album *Live-Evil* (1970) and the film sound track *A Tribute to Jack Johnson* (1970) being particular highlights.

Legacy

Davis was injured in an auto accident in 1972, curtailing his activities, then retired from 1975 through 1980. He returned to public notice with *The Man with the Horn* (1981) and subsequently dabbled in a variety of musical styles, concentrating mostly on jazz-rock dance music, but there were also notable experiments in other styles. Davis won several Grammy Awards during this period for such albums as *We Want Miles* (1982), *Tutu* (1986), and *Aura* (1989). One of the most-memorable events of Davis's later years occurred at the Montreux Jazz Festival in 1991, when he joined with an orchestra conducted by Quincy Jones to perform some of the classic Gil Evans arrangements of the late 1950s. Davis died less than three months later. His final album, *Doo-Bop* (1992), was released posthumously.

CHUCK BERRY

(b. Oct. 18, 1926, St. Louis, Mo., U.S.—d. March 18, 2017, Wentzville, Mo.)

Singer, songwriter, and guitarist Chuck Berry (born Charles Edward Anderson Berry) was one of the most popular and influential performers in rhythm-and-blues and rock-and-roll music in the 1950s, '60s, and '70s.

Raised in a working-class African American neighbourhood on the north side of the highly segregated city of St. Louis, Berry grew up in a family proud of its African-American and Native American ancestry. He gained early exposure to music through his family's participation in the choir of the Antioch Baptist Church, through the blues and country western music he heard on the radio, and through music classes, especially at Sumner High School. Berry was still attending high school when he was sent to serve three years for armed robbery at a Missouri prison for young offenders. After his release and return to St. Louis, he worked at an auto plant, studied hairdressing, and played music in small nightclubs. Berry traveled to Chicago in search of a recording contract; he signed with the Chess label, and in 1955 his first recording session produced "Maybellene," which stayed on the pop charts for 11 weeks, cresting at number five. Berry followed this success with extensive tours and hit after hit, including "Roll Over Beethoven" (1956), "Rock and Roll Music" (1957), and "Johnny B. Goode" (1958). His vivid descriptions of consumer culture and teenage life, the distinctive sounds he coaxed from his guitar, and the rhythmic and melodic virtuosity of his piano player (Johnny Johnson) made Berry's songs staples in the repertoire of almost every rock-and-roll band.

At the peak of his popularity, federal authorities prosecuted Berry for violating the Mann Act, alleging that he transported an underage female across state lines "for immoral purposes." After two trials tainted by racist overtones, Berry was convicted and remanded to prison. Upon his release he placed new hits on the pop charts, including "No Particular Place to Go" in 1964, at the height of the British Invasion, whose prime movers, the Beatles and the Rolling Stones, were hugely influenced by Berry (as were the Beach Boys). In 1972 Berry achieved his first number one hit, "My Ding-A-Ling." Although he recorded more sporadically in the 1970s and '80s, he continued to appear in concert, most often performing with backing bands comprising local musicians. Berry's public visibility increased in 1987 with the publication of his book *Chuck Berry: The Autobiography* and the release of the documentary film *Hail! Hail! Rock 'n' Roll*, featuring footage from his 60th birthday concert and guest appearances by Keith Richards and Bruce Springsteen.

Berry is undeniably one of the most influential figures in the history of rock music. In helping to create rock and roll from the crucible of rhythm and blues, he combined clever lyrics, distinctive guitar sounds, boogie-woogie rhythms, precise diction, an astounding stage show, and musical devices characteristic of country western music and the blues in his many best-selling single records and albums. A distinctive if not technically dazzling guitarist, Berry used electronic effects to replicate the ringing sounds of bottleneck blues guitarists in his recordings. He drew upon a broad range of musical genres in his compositions, displaying an especially strong interest in Caribbean music on "Havana Moon" (1957) and "Man and the Donkey" (1963), among others. Influenced by a wide variety of artists—including guitar players Carl Hogan, Charlie Christian, and T-Bone Walker and vocalists Nat King Cole, Louis Jordan, and Charles Brown—Berry played a major role in broadening the appeal of rhythm-and-blues music during the 1950s. He fashioned his lyrics to appeal to the growing teenage market by presenting vivid and humorous descriptions of high-school life, teen dances, and consumer culture. Many popular-music performers have recorded Berry's songs.

An appropriate tribute to Berry's centrality to rock and roll came when his song "Johnny B. Goode" was among the pieces of music placed on a copper phonograph record attached to the side of the Voyager 1 satellite, hurtling through outer space, in order to give distant or future civilizations a chance to acquaint themselves with the culture of the planet Earth in the 20th century. In 1984 he was presented with a Grammy Award for lifetime achievement. He was inducted into the Rock and Roll Hall of Fame in 1986.

ANTONIO CARLOS JOBIM
(b. Jan. 25, 1927, Rio de Janeiro, Braz.—d. Dec. 8, 1994, New York, N.Y., U.S.)

Brazilian songwriter, composer, and arranger Antonio Carlos Jobim transformed the extroverted rhythms of the Brazilian samba into an intimate music, the bossa nova ("new wrinkle" or "new wave"), which became internationally popular in the 1960s.

"Tom" Jobim—as he was popularly known—first began playing piano when he was 14 years old, on an instrument given to his sister by their stepfather. He quickly showed an aptitude for music, and his stepfather sent him to a series of highly accomplished classically trained musicians for lessons. During the course of his studies, Jobim was particularly inspired by the music of Brazilian composer Heitor Villa-Lobos (1887–1959), whose Western classical works regularly employed Brazilian melodic and rhythmic materials. When it came time to choose a career, Jobim initially showed no interest in pursuing music professionally, opting instead to become an architect. He soon became disenchanted with the choice, however, and left the field to devote himself fully to music.

Jobim subsequently performed in the clubs of Rio de Janeiro, transcribed songs for composers who could not write music, and arranged music for various recording artists before becoming music director of Odeon Records, one of the largest record companies in Brazil. In 1958 he began collaborating with singer-guitarist João Gilberto, whose recording of Jobim's song "Chega de Saudade" (1958; "No More Blues") is widely recognized as the first bossa nova single. Although the song itself met a cold reception, the bossa nova album that bears its name— *Chega de Saudade* (1959)—took Brazil by storm the following year. Also in 1959, Jobim and composer Luís Bonfá became noted for their collaboration with lyricist Vinícius de Moraes on the score for *Orfeo negro* (*Black Orpheus*), which won an Academy Award for best foreign film. By the early 1960s, Jobim's music was being played around the world.

Jobim maintained a second home in the United States, where bossa nova's fusion of understated samba pulse (quiet percussion and unamplified guitars playing subtly complex rhythms) and gentle, breathy singing with the melodious and sophisticated harmonic progressions of cool jazz found a long-lasting niche in popular music. In 1962 he appeared at Carnegie Hall with his leading jazz interpreters, tenor saxophonist Stan Getz and guitarist Charlie Byrd. Jobim collaborated on many albums, such as *Getz/Gilberto* (1963) and *Frank Sinatra & Antonio Carlos Jobim* (1967). He also recorded solo albums, most notably *Jobim* (1972) and *A Certain Mr. Jobim* (1965), and composed classical works and film scores. Of the more than 400 songs Jobim produced in the course of his musical career, "Samba de uma nota só" ("One-Note Samba"), "Desafinado" ("Slightly

Out of Tune"), "Meditação" ("Meditation"), "Corcovado" ("Quiet Nights of Quiet Stars"), "Garota de Ipanema" ("The Girl from Ipanema"), "Wave," and "Dindi" have been particularly popular.

RAY CHARLES

(b. Sept. 23, 1930, Albany, Ga., U.S.—d. June 10, 2004, Beverly Hills, Calif.)

American pianist, singer, composer, and bandleader Ray Charles Robinson was a leading entertainer, often billed as "the Genius." Charles was credited with the early development of soul music, a style based on a melding of gospel, rhythm and blues, and jazz music.

When Charles was an infant his family moved to Greenville, Florida, and he began his musical career at age five on a piano in a neighbourhood café. He began to go blind at six, possibly from glaucoma, completely losing his sight by age seven. He attended the St. Augustine School for the Deaf and Blind, where he concentrated on musical studies, but left school at age 15 to play the piano professionally after his mother died from cancer (his father had died when the boy was 10).

Charles built a remarkable career based on the immediacy of emotion in his performances. After emerging as a blues and jazz pianist indebted to Nat King Cole's style in the late 1940s, Charles recorded the boogie-woogie classic *"Mess Around"* and the novelty song "It Should've Been Me" in 1952–53. His arrangement for Guitar Slim's "The Things That I Used to Do" became a blues million-seller in 1953. By 1954 Charles had created a successful combination of blues and gospel influences and signed on with Atlantic Records. Propelled by Charles's distinctive raspy voice, "I've Got a Woman" and "Hallelujah I Love You So" became hit records. "What'd I Say" led the

Ray Charles, pictured in 1969, won 13 Grammy Awards during his career.

rhythm-and-blues sales charts in 1959 and was Charles's own first million-seller.

Charles's rhythmic piano playing and band arranging revived the "funky" quality of jazz, but he also recorded in many other musical genres. He entered the pop market with the best-sellers "Georgia on My Mind" (1960) and "Hit the Road, Jack" (1961). His album *Modern Sounds in Country and Western Music* (1962) sold more than one million copies, as did its single, "I Can't Stop Loving You." Thereafter his music emphasized jazz standards and renditions of pop and show tunes.

From 1955 Charles toured extensively in the United States and elsewhere with his own big band and a gospel-style female backup quartet called The Raeletts. He also appeared on television and worked in films such as *Ballad in Blue* (1964) and *The Blues Brothers* (1980) as a featured act and sound track composer. He formed his own custom recording labels, Tangerine in 1962 and Crossover Records in 1973. The recipient of many national and international awards, he received 13 Grammy Awards, including a lifetime achievement award in 1987. In 1986 Charles was inducted into the Rock and Roll Hall of Fame and received a Kennedy Center Honor. He published an autobiography, *Brother Ray, Ray Charles' Own Story* (1978), written with David Ritz.

PATSY CLINE

(b. Sept. 8, 1932, Winchester, Va., U.S.—d. March 5, 1963, near Camden, Tenn.)

American country and western singer Patsy Cline (born Virginia Patterson Hensley) helped bridge the gap between country music and more mainstream audiences.

Known in her youth as "Ginny," she began to sing with local country bands while a teenager, sometimes accompanying herself on guitar. By the time she had reached her early 20s, Cline was promoting herself as "Patsy" and was on her way toward country music stardom. She first recorded on the Four Star label in 1955, but it was with the advent of television culture in the late 1950s that she gained a wider audience. Cline began appearing on the radio and on *Town and Country Jamboree*, a local television variety show that was broadcast every Saturday night from Capitol Arena in Washington, D.C.

Singing "Walkin' After Midnight" as a contestant on the CBS television show *Arthur Godfrey's Talent Scouts*, Cline took first prize—the opportunity to appear on Godfrey's morning show for two weeks. She thereby gained national exposure both for herself and for her song. Three years later she became a regular performer on the Grand Ole Opry radio broadcasts from Nashville, Tenn., which largely defined the country music genre. Although Cline preferred traditional country music, which typically included vocalizations such as yodeling, the country music industry—coming into increasing competition with rock and roll—was trying to increase its appeal to a more mainstream audience. After her recording of "I Fall to Pieces" remained a popular seller for 39 consecutive weeks, she was marketed as a pop singer and was backed by strings and vocals. Cline never fully donned the pop music mantle, however: she did not eliminate yodeling from her repertoire, she dressed in distinctly western-style clothing, and she favoured country songs—especially heart-wrenching ballads of lost or waning love—over her three popular songs "Walkin' After Midnight," "I Fall to Pieces," and "Crazy" (written by a young Willie Nelson).

Cline's life was cut short in March 1963 by an airplane crash that also killed fellow entertainers Cowboy Copas and Hawkshaw Hawkins. In her short career, however, she helped usher in the modern era for American country singers; she figures prominently, for instance, as singer

Loretta Lynn's mentor in Lynn's autobiography, *Coal Miner's Daughter* (1976). Cline was elected to the Country Music Hall of Fame in 1973.

JAMES BROWN
(b. May 3, 1933, Barnwell, S.C., U.S.—d. Dec. 25, 2006, Atlanta, Ga.)

Known as "the Godfather of Soul," American singer, songwriter, arranger, and dancer James Brown was one of the most important and influential entertainers in 20th-century popular music. His remarkable achievements earned him the sobriquet "the Hardest-Working Man in Show Business."

Brown was raised mainly in Augusta, Ga., by his great-aunt, who took him in at about the age of five when his parents divorced. Growing up in the segregated South during the Great Depression of the 1930s, Brown was so impoverished that he was sent home from grade school for "insufficient clothes," an experience that he never forgot and that perhaps explains his penchant as an adult for wearing ermine coats, velour jumpsuits, elaborate capes, and conspicuous gold jewelry. Neighbours taught him how to play drums, piano, and guitar, and he learned about gospel music in churches and at tent revivals, where preachers would scream, yell, stomp their feet, and fall to their knees during sermons to provoke responses from the congregation.

At age 15 Brown and some companions were arrested while breaking into cars. He was sentenced to 8 to 16 years of incarceration but was released after 3 years for good behaviour. While at the Alto Reform School, he formed a gospel group. Subsequently secularized and renamed the Flames (later the Famous Flames), it soon attracted the attention of rhythm-and-blues and rock-and-roll shouter Little Richard, whose manager helped promote the group. Intrigued by their demo record, Ralph Bass, the artists-and-repertoire man for the King label, brought the group to Cincinnati, Ohio, to record for King Records' subsidiary Federal. Brown's first recording, "Please, Please, Please" (1956) eventually sold three million copies and launched his extraordinary career. Along with placing nearly 100 singles and almost 50 albums on the best-seller charts, Brown broke new ground with two of the first successful "live and in concert" albums—his landmark *Live at the Apollo* (1963), and his 1964 follow-up, *Pure Dynamite! Live at the Royal*.

During the 1960s Brown was known as "Soul Brother Number One." His hit recordings of that decade have often been associated with the emergence of the black aesthetic and black nationalist movements, especially the songs "Say It Loud—I'm Black and I'm Proud" (1968), "Don't Be a Drop-Out" (1966), and "I Don't Want Nobody to Give Me Nothin' (Open Up the Door, I'll Get It Myself)" (1969). In the 1970s Brown became "the Godfather of Soul," and his hit songs stimulated several dance crazes and were featured on the sound tracks of a number of "blaxploitation" films (sensational, low-budget, action-oriented motion pictures with African American protagonists). When hip-hop emerged as a viable commercial music in the 1980s, Brown's songs again assumed centre stage as hip-hop disc jockeys frequently incorporated samples (audio snippets) from his records. He also appeared in several motion pictures, including *The Blues Brothers* (1980) and *Rocky IV* (1985), and attained global status as a celebrity, especially in Africa, where his tours attracted enormous crowds and generated a broad range of new musical fusions. Yet Brown's life continued to be marked by difficulties, including the tragic death of his third wife, charges of drug use, and a period of imprisonment for a 1988 high-speed highway chase in which he tried to escape pursuing police officers.

Brown's uncanny ability to "scream" on key, to sing soulful slow ballads as well as electrifying up-tempo tunes, to plumb the rhythmic possibilities of the human voice and instrumental accompaniment, and to blend blues, gospel, jazz, and country vocal styles together made him one of the most influential vocalists of the 20th century. His extraordinary dance routines featuring deft deployment of microphones and articles of clothing as props, acrobatic leaps, full-impact knee landings, complex rhythmic patterns, dazzling footwork, dramatic entrances, and melodramatic exits redefined public performance within popular music and inspired generations of imitators (not least Michael Jackson). His careful attention to every aspect of his shows, from arranging songs to supervising sidemen, from negotiating performance fees to selecting costumes, guaranteed his audiences a uniformly high level of professionalism every night and established a precedent in artistic autonomy. In the course of an extremely successful commercial career, Brown's name was associated with an extraordinary number and range of memorable songs, distinctive dance steps, formative fashion trends, and even significant social issues. A skilled dancer and singer with an extraordinary sense of timing, Brown played a major role in bringing rhythm to the foreground of popular music. In addition to providing melody and embellishment, the horn players in his bands functioned as a rhythm section (they had to think like drummers), and musicians associated with him (Jimmy Nolan, Bootsy Collins, Fred Wesley, and Maceo Parker) have played an important role in creating the core vocabulary and grammar of funk music. Brown was inducted into the Rock and Roll Hall of Fame in 1986.

ELVIS PRESLEY
(b. Jan. 8, 1935, Tupelo, Miss., U.S.—d. Aug. 16, 1977, Memphis, Tenn.)

American popular singer Elvis Aaron Presley, widely known as the "King of Rock and Roll," was one of rock music's dominant performers from the mid-1950s until his death.

Presley grew up dirt-poor in Tupelo, moved to Memphis as a teenager, and, with his family, was off welfare only a few weeks when producer Sam Phillips at Sun Records, a local blues label, responded to his audition tape with a phone call. Several weeks' worth of recording sessions ensued with a band consisting of Presley, guitarist Scotty Moore, and bassist Bill Black. Their repertoire consisted of the kind of material for which Presley would become famous: blues and country songs, Tin Pan Alley ballads, and gospel hymns. Presley knew some of this music from the radio, some of it from his parents' Pentecostal church and the group sings he attended at the Reverend H.W. Brewster's black Memphis church, and some of it from the Beale Street blues clubs he began frequenting as a teenager.

Presley was already a flamboyant personality, with relatively long greased-back hair and wild-coloured clothing combinations, but his full musical personality did not emerge until he and the band began playing with blues singer Arthur ("Big Boy") Crudup's song "That's All Right Mama" in July 1954. They arrived at a startling synthesis, eventually dubbed rockabilly, retaining many of the original's blues inflections but with Presley's high tenor voice adding a lighter touch and with the basic rhythm striking a much more supple groove. This sound was the hallmark of the five singles Presley released on Sun over the next year. Although none of them became a national hit, by August 1955, when he released the fifth, "Mystery Train," arguably his greatest record ever, he had attracted a substantial Southern following for his recordings, his live appearances in regional roadhouses and clubs, and his radio performances on the nationally aired *Louisiana Hayride*. (A key musical change came when drummer D.J. Fontana was added, first for the *Hayride* shows but also on records beginning with "Mystery Train.")

Presley's management was then turned over to Colonel Tom Parker, a country music hustler who had made stars of Eddy Arnold and Hank Snow. Parker arranged for Presley's song catalog and recording contract to be sold to major New York City-based enterprises, Hill and Range and RCA Victor, respectively. Sun received a total of $35,000; Elvis got $5,000. He began recording at RCA's studios in Nashville, Tennessee, with a somewhat larger group of musicians but still including Moore, Black, and Fontana and began to create a national sensation with a series of hits: "Heartbreak Hotel," "Don't Be Cruel," "Love Me Tender" (all 1956), "All Shook Up" (1957), and more.

From 1956 through 1958 Presley completely dominated the best-seller charts and ushered in the age of rock and roll, opening doors for both white and black rock artists. His television appearances, especially those on Ed Sullivan's Sunday night variety show, set records for the size of the audiences. Even his films, a few slight vehicles, were box office smashes.

Presley became the teen idol of his decade, greeted everywhere by screaming hordes of young women, and, when it was announced in early 1958 that he had been drafted and would enter the U.S. Army, there was that rarest of all pop culture events, a moment of true grief. More important, he served as the great cultural catalyst of his period. Elvis projected a mixed vision of humility and self-confidence, of intense commitment and comic

Elvis Presley is pictured in a 1957 promotional image for the movie Jailhouse Rock.

disbelief in his ability to create frenzy. He inspired literally thousands of musicians—initially those more or less like-minded Southerners, from Jerry Lee Lewis and Carl Perkins on down, who were the first generation of rockabillies, and, later, people who had far different combinations of musical and cultural influences and ambitions. From John Lennon to Bruce Springsteen, Bob Dylan to Prince, it was impossible to think of a rock star of any importance who did not owe an explicit debt to Presley.

Beyond even that, Presley inspired his audience. "It was like he whispered his dream in all our ears and then we dreamed it," said Springsteen at the time of Presley's death. You did not have to want to be a rock and roll star or even a musician to want to be like Elvis—which meant, ultimately, to be free and uninhibited and yet still a part of the everyday. Literally millions of people—an entire generation or two—defined their sense of personal style and ambition in terms that Elvis first personified.

As a result, he was anything but universally adored. Those who did not worship him found him despicable (no one found him ignorable). Preachers and pundits declared him an anathema, his Pentecostally derived hip-swinging stage style and breathy vocal asides obscene. Racists denounced him for mingling black music with white (and Presley was always scrupulous in crediting his black sources, one of the things that made him different from the Tin Pan Alley writers and singers who had for decades lifted black styles without credit). He was pronounced responsible for all teenage hooliganism and juvenile delinquency. Yet, in every appearance on television, he appeared affable, polite, and soft-spoken, almost shy. It was only with a band at his back and a beat in his ear that he became "Elvis the Pelvis."

In 1960 Presley returned from the army, where he had served as a soldier in Germany rather than joining the

Special Services entertainment division. Those who regarded him as commercial hype without talent expected him to fade away. Instead, he continued to have hits from recordings stockpiled just before he entered the army. Upon his return to the States, he picked up pretty much where he had left off, churning out a series of more than 30 movies (from *Blue Hawaii* to *Change of Habit*) over the next eight years, almost none of which fit any genre other than "Elvis movie," which meant a light comedic romance with musical interludes. Most had accompanying soundtrack albums, and together the movies and the records made him a rich man, although they nearly ruined him as any kind of artist. Presley did his best work in the 1960s on singles either unconnected to the films or only marginally stuck into them, recordings such as "It's Now or Never ('O Sole Mio')" (1960), "Are You Lonesome Tonight?," "Little Sister" (both 1961), "Can't Help Falling in Love," "Return to Sender" (both 1962), and "Viva Las Vegas" (1964). Presley was no longer a controversial figure; he had become one more predictable mass entertainer, a personage of virtually no interest to the rock audience that had expanded so much with the advent of the new sounds of the Beatles, the Rolling Stones, and Dylan.

By 1968 the changes in the music world had overtaken Presley—both movie grosses and record sales had fallen. In December his one-man Christmas TV special aired; a tour de force of rock and roll and rhythm and blues, it restored much of his dissipated credibility. In 1969 he released a single having nothing to do with a film, "Suspicious Minds"; it went to number one. He also began doing concerts again and quickly won back a sizable following, although it was not nearly as universal as his audience in the 1950s. For much of the next decade, he was again one of the top live attractions in the United States. Presley was now a mainstream American entertainer, an icon but not so much an idol. He had married in 1967 without much furor, became a parent with the birth of his daughter, Lisa Marie, in 1968, and got divorced in 1973. He made no more movies, and his recordings were of uneven quality. Hits were harder to come by—"Suspicious Minds" was his last number one and "Burning Love" (1972) his final Top Ten entry. But, thanks to the concerts, spectaculars best described by critic Jon Landau as an apotheosis of American musical comedy, he remained a big money earner.

However, Presley had also developed a lethal lifestyle. Spending almost all his time when not on the road in Graceland, his Memphis estate, he lived nocturnally, surrounded by sycophants and stuffed with greasy foods and a variety of prescription drugs. His shows deteriorated in the final two years of his life, and his recording career came to a virtual standstill. Finally, in the summer of 1977, the night before he was to begin yet another concert tour, he died of a heart attack brought on largely by drug abuse. He was 42 years old.

LUCIANO PAVAROTTI
(b. Oct. 12, 1935, Modena, Italy—d. Sept. 6, 2007, Modena)

Italian operatic lyric tenor Luciano Pavarotti was considered one of the finest bel canto opera singers of the 20th century. Even in the highest register, his voice was noted for its purity of tone, and his concerts, recordings, and television appearances—which provided him ample opportunity to display his ebullient personality—gained him a wide popular following.

Pavarotti graduated from a teaching institute in Modena (1955) and then taught elementary school for two years. He studied opera privately, mostly in Mantua. After winning the Concorso Internazionale, a singing competition, he made his professional operatic debut in 1961 as Rodolfo in *La Bohème* (1896) in Reggio nell'Emilia, Italy.

He then played in opera houses throughout Europe and Australia and performed the role of Idamante in Mozart's *Idomeneo* (1781) at the Glyndebourne Festival in 1964. He made his first appearance in the United States in Miami in 1965, singing opposite Joan Sutherland as Edgardo in *Lucia di Lammermoor* (1835). In 1968 he made his debut at the Metropolitan Opera House in New York City, and from 1971 he was a regular performer there. Pavarotti toured the world, performing to as many as 500,000 fans at a time in outdoor venues, as a solo performer or as one of the "Three Tenors" (with Plácido Domingo and José Carreras). Among his many prizes and awards were five Grammy Awards and a Kennedy Center Honor in 2001.

His most notable operatic roles included the Duke in Giuseppe Verdi's *Rigoletto* (1851), Tonio in Gaetano Donizetti's *La Fille du régiment* (1840; a part remarkable for its demanding sequence of high Cs), Arturo in Vincenzo Bellini's *I puritani* (1835), and Radamès in Verdi's *Aida* (1871), all of which are available as sound recordings. He performed in a number of televised opera broadcasts. In addition to his opera work, Pavarotti also recorded a collection of Italian love songs (*Amore* [1992; "Love"]) and a pop album (*Ti adoro* [2003; "I Adore You"]).

With William Wright he wrote *Pavarotti: My Own Story* (1981) and *Pavarotti: My World* (1995). In 2004 Pavarotti gave his final performance on the operatic stage, although he continued to sing publicly until 2006. His last public appearance was in the opening ceremony of the 2006 Winter Olympics in Turin, Italy, where he sang his signature aria, *Nessun dorma*, from Giacomo Puccini's *Turandot* (first performed 1926).

BUDDY HOLLY

(b. Sept. 7, 1936, Lubbock, Texas, U.S. — d. Feb. 3, 1959, near Clear Lake, Iowa)

American singer and songwriter Charles Hardin Holley, professionally known as Buddy Holly, produced some of the most distinctive and influential work in rock music.

Holly (the *e* was dropped from his last name — probably accidentally — on his first record contract) was the youngest of four children in a family of devout Baptists in the West Texas town of Lubbock, and gospel music was an important part of his life from an early age. A good student possessed of infectious personal charm, Holly was declared "King of the Sixth Grade" by his classmates. He became seriously interested in music at about age 12 and pursued it with remarkable natural ability.

The African American rhythm and blues that Holly heard on the radio had a tremendous impact on him, as it did on countless other white teenagers in the racially segregated United States of the 1950s. Already well versed in country music, bluegrass, and gospel and a seasoned performer by age 16, he became a rhythm-and-blues devotee. By 1955, after hearing Elvis Presley, Holly was a full-time rock and roller. Late that year he bought a Fender Stratocaster electric guitar and developed a style of playing featuring ringing major chords that became his trademark. In 1956 he signed with Decca Records' Nashville, Tennessee, division, but the records he made for them were uneven in quality, and most sold poorly.

In 1957 Holly and his new group, the Crickets (Niki Sullivan on second guitar and background vocals, Joe B. Mauldin on bass, and the great Jerry Allison on drums), began their association with independent producer

Norman Petty at his studio in Clovis, New Mexico. Together they created a series of recordings that display an emotional intimacy and sense of detail that set them apart from other 1950s rock and roll. As a team, they threw away the rule book and let their imaginations loose. Unlike most independent rock-and-roll producers of the time, Petty did not own any cheap equipment. He wanted his recordings to sound classy and expensive, but he also loved to experiment and had a deep bag of sonic tricks. The Crickets' records feature unusual microphone placement techniques, imaginative echo chamber effects, and overdubbing, a process that in the 1950s meant superimposing one recording on another. While crafting tracks such as "Not Fade Away," "Peggy Sue," "Listen to Me," and "Everyday," Holly and the Crickets camped out at Petty's studio for days at a time, using it as a combination laboratory and playground. They were the first rock and rollers to approach the recording process in this manner.

When the Crickets' first single, "That'll Be the Day," was released in 1957, their label, Brunswick, did nothing to promote it. Nevertheless, the record had an irrepressible spirit, and by year's end it became an international multi-million-seller. Soon after, Holly became a star and an icon. Holly and the Crickets' association with Petty (who, serving as their manager, songwriting partner, and publisher, owned their recordings) was far from all beneficial, however. According to virtually all accounts, Petty collected the Crickets' royalty checks and kept the money. By 1959 the hit records tapered off, and Holly was living in New York with his new bride. Estranged from the Crickets and broke, he was also contemplating legal action against Petty. This left him little choice but to participate in the doomed "Winter Dance Party of 1959" tour through the frozen Midwest, during which he and coheadliners Ritchie Valens and the

Big Bopper (J.P. Richardson) were killed in a plane crash.

The music of Holly and the Crickets, their innovative use of the studio, and the fact that they wrote most of their songs themselves made them the single most important influence on the Beatles, who knew every Holly record backward and forward. In 1986 Holly was inducted into the Rock and Roll Hall of Fame, and in 1996 he was honoured by the National Academy of Recording Arts and Sciences with a lifetime achievement award.

THE ROLLING STONES

The original members were Mick Jagger (b. July 26, 1943, Dartford, Kent, Eng.), Keith Richards (b. Dec. 18, 1943, Dartford, Kent, Eng.), Brian Jones (b. Feb. 28, 1942, Cheltenham, Gloucestershire, Eng.—d. July 3, 1969, Hartfield, Sussex), Bill Wyman (b. Oct. 24, 1936, London, Eng.), and Charlie Watts (b. June 2, 1941, London, Eng.—d. Aug. 24, 2021, London, Eng.). Later members were Mick Taylor (b. Jan. 17, 1948, Hereford, East Hereford and Worcester, Eng.), Ron Wood (b. June 1, 1947, London, Eng.), and Darryl Jones (b. Dec. 11, 1961, Chicago, Ill., U.S.).

Formed in 1962, the Rolling Stones are a British rock group that has drawn on Chicago blues stylings to create a unique vision of the dark side of post-1960s counterculture.

No rock band has sustained consistent activity and global popularity for so long a period as the Rolling Stones, still capable, more than 45 years after their formation, of filling the largest stadia in the world. Though several of their mid-1960s contemporaries—notably Bob Dylan, Paul McCartney, Eric Clapton, and Van Morrison—have maintained individual positions in rock's front line, the Rolling Stones' nucleus of singer Jagger, guitarist Richards, and drummer Watts remains rock's most durable ongoing partnership.

In the process, the Stones have become rock's definitive, emblematic band: a seamless blend of sound, look, and public image. That they are the mold from which various generations of challengers have been struck—from the Who, Led Zeppelin, and Aerosmith (via the New York Dolls), the Clash, the Sex Pistols all the way to Guns N' Roses and Oasis—is virtually inarguable. In their onstage personae, Jagger and Richards established the classic rock band archetypes: the preening, narcissistic singer and the haggard, obsessive guitarist.

Formed in London as an alliance between Jagger, Richards, and multi-instrumentalist Brian Jones along with Watts and bassist Wyman, the Stones began as a grubby conclave of students and bohemians playing a then-esoteric music based on Chicago ghetto blues in pubs and clubs in and around West London. Their potential for mass-market success seemed negligible at first, but by 1965 they were second only to the Beatles in the collective affection of teenage Britain. However, whereas the Beatles of the mid-1960s had longish hair, wore matching suits, and appeared utterly charming, the Stones had considerably longer hair, all dressed differently, and seemed thoroughly intimidating. As the Beatles grew ever more respectable and reassuring, the Stones became correspondingly more rebellious and threatening. The Stones—specifically Jagger, Richards, and Jones—were subjected to intense police and press harassment for drug use and all-purpose degeneracy, whereas the Beatles, who were in private life no less fond of marijuana, sex, and alcohol, were welcomed at Buckingham Palace and made Members of the Order of the British Empire (M.B.E.) by the queen.

The Stones' early repertoire consisted primarily of recycled gems from the catalogs of the blues and rock-and-roll titans of the 1950s: their first five singles and the bulk of their first two albums were composed by others. The turning point was reached when, spurred on by the example of the Beatles' John Lennon and Paul McCartney, Jagger and Richards began composing their own songs, which not only ensured the long-term viability of the band but also served to place the Jagger-Richards team firmly in creative control of the group. Jones had been their prime motivating force in their early days, and he was the band's most gifted instrumentalist as well as its prettiest face, but he had little talent for composition and became increasingly marginalized. His textural wizardry dominated their first all-original album, *Aftermath* (1966), which featured him on marimba, dulcimer, sitar, and assorted keyboards as well as on his customary guitar and harmonica. Thereafter, however, he declined in both creativity and influence, becoming a depressive, drug-sodden liability eventually fired by the band mere weeks before his death.

The Jagger-Richards songwriting team created its first bona fide classic, "(I Can't Get No) Satisfaction," in 1965 and enjoyed a string of innovative hit singles well into 1966, including "Paint It Black," "19th Nervous Breakdown," "Get off My Cloud," "Have You Seen Your Mother, Baby," and "Lady Jane," but the era of art-pop and psychedelia, which coincided with the Beatles' creative peak, represented a corresponding trough for the Stones. The fashions of the era of whimsy and flower power did not suit their essentially dark and disruptive energies, and their psychedelic album *Their Satanic Majesties Request* (1967) contributed little beyond its title to their legend. Furthermore, they were hampered by seemingly spending as much time in court and jail as they did in the studio or on tour. However, as the mood of the time darkened, the Stones hit a new stride in 1968 with the epochal single "Jumpin' Jack Flash," which reconnected them to their blues-rock roots, and the album *Beggars Banquet*. Replacing

Mick Jagger of the Rolling Stones performs in The Hague, Netherlands, in 1976.

Jones with the virtuosic but self-effacing guitarist Mick Taylor, they returned to the road in 1969, almost instantly becoming rock's premier touring attraction.

By the end of 1970 the Beatles had broken up, Jimi Hendrix was dead, and Led Zeppelin had barely appeared on the horizon. Though Led Zeppelin eventually outsold the Stones by five albums to one, no group could challenge their central position in the rock pantheon. Moreover, the death of Brian Jones combined with Taylor's lack of onstage presence elevated public perception of Richards's status from that of Jagger's right-hand man to effective coleader of the band.

The period between "Jumpin' Jack Flash" and the double album *Exile on Main Street* (1972) remains their creative and iconic peak. Including the studio albums *Let It Bleed* (1969) and *Sticky Fingers* (1971) plus the in-concert *Get Yer Ya-Yas Out!* (1970), it gave them the repertoire and image that still defines them and on which they have continued to trade ever since: an incendiary blend of sex, drugs, satanism, and radical politics delivered with their patented fusion of Jagger's ironic distance and Richards's tatterdemalion intensity. Their records and concerts at this time both explored and provided the soundtrack for the contradictions of a collapsing counterculture at a time when almost everybody else still seemed to be in a state of psychedelic euphoria.

Their recordings of this period found them adding country music to their list of influences and—most notably on *Beggars Banquet*—adding more and more acoustic guitar textures to their already impressive command of musical light and shade. Yet their blues-powered foray into the era's heart of darkness bore bitter fruit indeed: when a young black man was murdered by Hell's Angels at a disastrous free concert at the Altamont Speedway in Livermore,

Calif., during their 1969 American tour, it seemed to many observers that the Stones' own aura of decadence and danger was somehow to blame for the tragedy.

The quality of their music began to decline after *Exile on Main Street*. Jagger and Richards began to act out the group's fascination with the juxtaposition of high society and lowlife: the singer became a jet-set figure; the guitarist, a full-time junkie who finally "cleaned up" in 1977 and thereby saved both his own life and the band's future. Taylor left in 1975 to be replaced by Wood, formerly of the Faces, and, despite the occasional bright spot like *Some Girls* (1978), *Emotional Rescue* (1980), or "Start Me Up" (1981), the Stones' albums and singles became increasingly predictable, though their tours continued to sell out. Both Jagger and Richards recorded solo albums that performed relatively poorly in the marketplace, though Richards's work was significantly more favourably reviewed than Jagger's.

The Stones embarked on their *Steel Wheels* album and tour in 1989. Wyman retired in 1992 and was replaced on tour by Daryl Jones, formerly a bassist for Miles Davis and Sting, and in the studio by a variety of guest musicians. Jagger, Richards, and Wood continue to trade as the Rolling Stones, and, whenever they tour, audiences flock in the thousands to discover if the old lions can still roar.

Several prominent directors have sought to translate the electricity of the Stones as live performers to the screen, including Jean-Luc Godard, with the impressionistic *Sympathy for the Devil* (1968); Hal Ashby, with *Let's Spend the Night Together* (1982); and, perhaps most notably, David Maysles, Albert Maysles, and Charlotte Zwerin, with *Gimme Shelter* (1970), which covered the group's 1969 tour and Altamont Speedway concert. More recently, in the wake of the group's well-received album *A Bigger Bang* (2005), director Martin Scorsese, long a fan of the group, focused less on the spectacle of a Stones' concert and more on the band as performers. The result, *Shine a Light* (2008), met with critical acclaim and confirmed that the Rolling Stones remained a major presence in the rock scene of the 21st century.

PHILIP GLASS
(b. Jan. 31, 1937, Baltimore, Md., U.S.)

Philip Glass is an American composer of innovative instrumental, vocal, and operatic music, who variously has employed minimalist, atonal, and non-Western elements in his work.

Glass studied flute as a boy and enrolled at age 15 at the University of Chicago, where he studied mathematics and philosophy and graduated in 1956. His interest in atonal music drew him on to study composition at the Juilliard School of Music (M.S., 1962) in New York City and then to Paris to study under Nadia Boulanger. His acquaintance there with the Indian sitarist Ravi Shankar decisively affected Glass's compositional style, and he temporarily jettisoned such traditional formal qualities as harmony, tempo, and melody in his music. Instead he began creating ensemble pieces in a monotonous and repetitive style; these works consisted of a series of syncopated rhythms ingeniously contracted or extended within a stable diatonic structure. Such minimalist music, played by a small ensemble using electronically amplified keyboard and wind instruments, earned Glass a small but enthusiastic following in New York City by the late 1960s.

Glass's opera *Einstein on the Beach* (1976), composed in collaboration with Robert Wilson, earned him broader acclaim; this work showed a renewed interest in classical Western harmonic elements, though his interest in startling rhythmic and melodic changes remained the work's most dramatic feature. Glass's opera *Satyagraha* (1980) was a more authentically "operatic" portrayal of incidents from the early life of Mohandas K. Gandhi. In this work, the dronelike repetition of symmetrical sequences of chords attained a haunting and hypnotic power well attuned to the religio-spiritual themes of the libretto, adapted from the Hindu scripture the *Bhagavadgītā*. The opera *The Voyage* (1992) had mixed reviews, but the fact that it had been commissioned by the New York Metropolitan Opera (to commemorate the 500th anniversary of Christopher Columbus's arrival in the Americas) confirmed Glass's growing acceptance by the classical music establishment.

SMOKEY ROBINSON AND THE MIRACLES

In addition to Smokey Robinson (b. Feb. 19, 1940, Detroit, Mich., U.S.), the principal members of the group were Warren Moore (b. Nov. 19, 1939, Detroit, Mich., U.S.—d. Nov. 19, 2017, Las Vegas, Nev.), Bobby Rogers (b. Feb. 19, 1940, Detroit, Mich., U.S.—d. March 3, 2013, Soutfield, Mich.), Ronnie White (b. April 5, 1939, Detroit, Mich., U.S.—d. Aug. 26, 1995, Detroit, Mich.), and Claudette Rogers (b. 1942)

Smokey Robinson and the Miracles were an American vocal group that helped define the Motown sound of the 1960s; the group was led by one of the most gifted, influential singer-songwriters in 20th-century popular music.

Whether writing for fellow artists Mary Wells, the Temptations, or Marvin Gaye or performing with the Miracles, singer-lyricist-arranger-producer Robinson created songs that were supremely balanced between the joy and pain of love. At once playful and passionate, Robinson's graceful lyrics led Bob Dylan to call him "America's greatest living poet."

Coming of age in the doo-wop era and deeply influenced by jazz vocalist Sarah Vaughan, Robinson formed the Five Chimes with school friends in the mid-1950s. After some personnel changes, the group, as the Matadors, auditioned unsuccessfully for Jackie Wilson's manager; however, they greatly impressed Wilson's songwriter Berry Gordy, who soon became their manager and producer. Most important, Gordy became Robinson's mentor, harnessing his prodigious but unformed composing talents, and Robinson, assisted by the Miracles, became Gordy's inspiration for the creation of Motown Records.

With the arrival of Claudette Rogers, the group changed its name to the Miracles and released "Got a Job" on End Records in 1958. The Miracles struggled onstage in their first performance at the Apollo Theatre that year, but good fortune came their way in the form of Marv Tarplin, guitarist for the Primettes, who were led by Robinson's friend Diana Ross. Tarplin became an honorary (but essential) Miracle, while Robinson introduced Gordy to the Primettes, who soon became the Supremes. In 1959 Robinson and Claudette Rogers were married, and "Bad Girl," licensed to Chess Records, peaked nationally at number 93. The fiery "Way Over There" and the shimmering "(You Can) Depend on Me" were followed in 1960 by "Shop Around," the second version of which became an enormous hit, reaching number one on the rhythm-and-blues charts and number two on the pop charts.

While Robinson was writing such vital songs as "My Guy" for Mary Wells, "I'll Be Doggone" for Marvin Gaye, and "My Girl" for the Temptations, he and the Miracles proceeded to record stunning compositions, including "You've Really Got a Hold on Me" (1962), "I'll Try Something New" (1962), "Ooo Baby Baby" (1965), "Choosey Beggar" (1965), "The Tracks of My Tears" (1965), and "More Love" (1967, written following the premature birth and death of Robinson's twin daughters). The Miracles complemented their songs of aching romance and mature love with buoyant numbers such as "Mickey's Monkey" (1963), "Going to a Go-Go" (1965), "I Second That Emotion" (1967), and "The Tears of a Clown" (1970).

In 1972 Robinson left the Miracles to pursue a solo career. Without him, the Miracles enjoyed moderate success in subsequent years (the disco-era "Love Machine [Part 1]" hit number one on the pop charts in 1975), while Robinson produced such solo hits as "Cruisin'" (1979) and "Being with You" (1981). He also unintentionally inspired the new soul radio format that took its name from the title track of his 1975 conceptual album *A Quiet Storm*. Robinson was inducted into the Rock and Roll Hall of Fame in 1987.

PARLIAMENT-FUNKADELIC

The original members were George Clinton (b. July 22, 1941, Kannapolis, N.C., U.S.), Raymond Davis (b. March 29, 1940, Sumter, S.C., U.S.—d. July 5, 2005, New Brunswick, N.J.), Calvin Simon (b. May 22, 1942, Beckley, W.Va., U.S.—d. Jan. 6, 2022, San Antonio, Fla.), Fuzzy Haskins (b. June 8, 1941, Elkhorn, W.Va., U.S.—d. March 17, 2023, Grosse Pointe Woods, Mich.), and Grady Thomas (b. Jan. 5, 1941, Newark, N.J., U.S.). Later members included Michael Hampton (b. Nov. 15, 1956, Cleveland, Ohio, U.S.), Bernie Worrell (b. April 19, 1944, Long Beach, N.J., U.S.—d. June 24, 2016, Everson, Wash.), Billy Bass Nelson (b. Jan. 28, 1951, Plainfield, N.J., U.S.), Eddie Hazel (b. April 10, 1950, Brooklyn, N.Y., U.S.—d. Dec. 23, 1992), Tiki Fulwood (b. May 23, 1944, Philadelphia, Pa., U.S.—d. Oct. 29, 1979), Bootsy Collins (b. Oct. 26, 1951, Cincinnati, Ohio, U.S.), Fred Wesley (b. July 4, 1943, Columbus, Ga., U.S.), Maceo Parker (b. Feb. 14, 1943, Kinston, N.C., U.S.), Jerome Brailey (b. Aug. 20, 1950, Richmond, Va., U.S.), Garry Shider (b. July 24, 1953, Plainfield, N.J., U.S.—d. June 16, 2010, Great Upper Marlboro, Md.), Glen Goins (b. Jan. 2, 1954, Plainfield, N.J., U.S.—d. July 29, 1978, Plainfield), and Gary ("Mudbone") Cooper (b. Nov. 24, 1953, Washington, D.C., U.S.).

Parliament-Funkadelic, also known as P-Funk, was a massive group of performers that greatly influenced Black music in the 1970s.

The group scored 13 Top Ten rhythm-and-blues and pop hits from 1967 to 1983 (including six number one rhythm-and-blues hits) under a variety of names, including the Parliaments, Funkadelic, Bootsy's Rubber Band, and the Brides of Funkenstein, as well as under the name of its founding father, Clinton.

The band combined the hard rock of Jimi Hendrix, the funky rhythms of James Brown, and the showstopping style of Sly and the Family Stone to fashion an outrageous tribal funk experience. P-Funk emphasized the aesthetics of funk as a means of self-fulfillment; to "give up the funk" meant to achieve transcendence.

Organized and produced by Clinton, the original Parliaments began as a doo-wop quintet based in Plainfield. The group's first charting single, "(I Wanna) Testify," in 1967 led to their first tour, but legal problems that arose with the demise of their record company resulted in the loss of the group's name. Performing throughout the northeastern United States and recording in Detroit, the group began to emphasize its backing band, Funkadelic. Led by bassist Nelson, guitarist Hazel, drummer Fulwood, and classically trained keyboardist Worrell, Funkadelic incorporated the influence of amplified, psychedelic rock into its distinctive sound.

By 1970 Clinton was producing albums for both the renamed Parliament and Funkadelic—essentially the same entity recording for different labels. In the process he recruited key new performers: Collins on bass, Wesley on trombone, and Parker on saxophone (all from James Brown's band the JBs), along with drummer Brailey, vocalist Cooper, lead guitarist Hampton, and vocalist-guitarists Shider and Goins. Success came in 1976 with the release of

Parliament's album *Mothership Connection* and the single "Give Up the Funk (Tear the Roof Off the Sucker)," which earned a gold record. Other hit singles followed, including "Flash Light" (1977) by Parliament, "One Nation Under a Groove" (1978) by Funkadelic, and "Atomic Dog" (1982) by Clinton.

P-Funk reached its peak in the late 1970s, sporting a massive stage act (with more than 40 performers) that showcased Clinton's visionary album concepts, Collins's spectacular bass effects, and Worrell's synthesizer innovations. However, by the early 1980s the large overhead and multifaceted legal identity of the group led to a collapse of the enterprise.

P-Funk defined the dance music of its time and influenced a range of styles from hard rock to house music. The P-Funk catalog is among the most sampled by rap music producers. Parliament-Funkadelic was inducted into the Rock and Roll Hall of Fame in 1997.

THE BEATLES

The principal members were Paul McCartney (b. June 18, 1942, Liverpool, Merseyside, Eng.), John Lennon (b. Oct. 9, 1940, Liverpool, Merseyside, Eng.—d. Dec. 8, 1980, New York, N.Y., U.S.), George Harrison (b. Feb. 25, 1943, Liverpool, Merseyside, Eng.—d. Nov. 29, 2001, Los Angeles, Calif., U.S.), and Ringo Starr (b. July 7, 1940, Liverpool, Merseyside, Eng.). Other early members included Stuart Sutcliffe (b. June 23, 1940, Edinburgh, Scot.—d. April 10, 1962, Hamburg, W. Ger.) and Pete Best (b. Nov. 24, 1941, Madras [now Chennai], India).

The Beatles were a British musical quartet and a global cynosure for the hopes and dreams of a generation that came of age in the 1960s.

Formed around the nucleus of Lennon and McCartney, who first performed together in Liverpool in 1957, the group grew out of a shared enthusiasm for American rock and roll. Lennon, a guitarist and singer, and McCartney, a bassist and singer, were largely self-taught as musicians. Precocious composers, they gathered around themselves a changing cast of accompanists, adding by the end of 1957 Harrison, a lead guitarist, and then, in 1960 for several formative months, Sutcliffe, who brought into the band a brooding sense of Bohemian style. After dabbling in skiffle, a jaunty sort of folk music popular in Britain in the late 1950s, and assuming several different names (the Quarrymen, the Silver Beetles, and, finally, the Beatles), the band added a drummer, Best, and joined a small but booming "beat music" scene.

In autumn 1961 Brian Epstein, a local Liverpool record store manager, saw the band, fell in love, became their manager, and proceeded to bombard the major British music companies with letters and tape recordings of the band. The group finally won a contract with Parlophone, a subsidiary of the giant EMI group of music labels. The man in charge of their career at Parlophone was George Martin, a classically trained musician who from the start put his stamp on the Beatles, first by suggesting the band hire a more polished drummer (they chose Starr) and then by rearranging their second recorded song (and first big British hit), "Please Please Me."

Throughout the winter and into the spring of 1963, the Beatles continued their rise to fame in England by producing spirited recordings of original tunes and also by playing classic American rock and roll on a variety of radio programs. In these months, fascination with the Beatles breached the normal barriers of taste, class, and age, transforming their recordings and live performances into matters of widespread public comment. In the fall of that year, when they made a couple of appearances on British television, the evidence of popular frenzy

The Beatles

The Beatles made several appearances on The Ed Sullivan Show.

prompted British newspapermen to coin a new word for the phenomenon: *Beatlemania*. In early 1964, after equally tumultuous appearances on American television, the same phenomenon erupted in the United States and provoked a so-called British Invasion of Beatles imitators from the United Kingdom.

Beatlemania was something new. Musicians performing in the 19th century certainly excited a frenzy, but that was before the mass media created the possibility of collective frenzy. Later pop music idols sold similarly large numbers of records, but without provoking anything approaching the hysteria caused by the Beatles. By the summer of 1964, when the Beatles appeared in *A Hard Day's Night*, a movie that dramatized the phenomenon of Beatlemania, the band's effect was evident around the world.

The popular hubbub convinced Lennon and McCartney of their songwriting abilities and sparked an outpouring of creative experimentation all but unprecedented in the history of rock music. Between 1965 and 1967 the music of the Beatles rapidly changed and evolved, becoming ever more subtle, sophisticated, and varied. Their repertoire in these years ranged from the chamber pop ballad "Yesterday" and the enigmatic folk tune "Norwegian Wood" (both in 1965) to the hallucinatory hard rock song "Tomorrow Never Knows" (1966), with a lyric inspired by Timothy Leary's handbook *The Psychedelic Experience* (1964). It also included the carnivalesque soundscape of "Being for the Benefit of Mr. Kite!" (1967), which featured stream-of-consciousness lyrics by Lennon and a typically imaginative arrangement (by Martin) built around randomly spliced-together snippets of recorded steam organs.

In 1966 the Beatles announced their retirement from public performing to concentrate on exploiting the full resources of the recording studio. A year later, in June

1967, this period of widely watched creative renewal was climaxed by the release of *Sgt. Pepper's Lonely Hearts Club Band*, an album avidly greeted by young people around the world as indisputable evidence not only of the band's genius but also of the era's utopian promise. More than a band of musicians, the Beatles had come to personify, certainly in the minds of millions of young listeners, the joys of a new counterculture of hedonism and uninhibited experimentation.

In those years the Beatles effectively reinvented the meaning of rock and roll as a cultural form. The American artists they chose to emulate—including Chuck Berry, Little Richard, Elvis Presley, the Everly Brothers, Buddy Holly, the rock composers Jerry Leiber and Mike Stoller, and, after 1964, folksinger Bob Dylan, among others—became widely regarded as canonic sources of inspiration, offering "classical" models for aspiring younger rock musicians. At the same time, the original songs the Beatles wrote and recorded dramatically expanded the musical range and expressive scope of the genre they had inherited.

After 1968 and the eruption of student protest movements in countries as different as Mexico and France, the Beatles insensibly surrendered their role as de facto leaders of an inchoate global youth culture. They nevertheless continued for several more years to record and release new music and maintained a level of popularity rarely rivaled before or since. The band continued to enjoy widespread popularity. The following year *Abbey Road* went on to become one of the band's best-loved and biggest-selling albums.

Meanwhile, personal disagreements magnified by the stress of symbolizing the dreams of a generation had begun to tear the band apart. Lennon and McCartney fell into bickering and mutual accusations of ill will, and in the spring of 1970 the Beatles formally disbanded. In the years that followed, all four members went on to produce solo albums of variable quality and popularity. Lennon released a corrosive set of songs with his new wife, Yoko Ono, and McCartney went on to form a band, Wings, that turned out a fair number of commercially successful recordings in the 1970s. Starr and Harrison, too, initially had some success as solo artists.

In 1980 Lennon was murdered by a demented fan outside the Dakota, an apartment building in New York City known for its celebrity tenants. The event provoked a global outpouring of grief. Lennon is memorialized in Strawberry Fields, a section of Central Park across from the Dakota that Yoko Ono landscaped in her husband's honour.

In the years that followed, the surviving former Beatles continued to record and perform as solo artists. McCartney in particular remained musically active, both in the pop field, producing new albums every few years, and in the field of classical music—in 1991 he completed *Liverpool Oratorio*; and in 1999 he released a new classical album, *Working Classical*. McCartney was knighted by the queen of England in 1997. Starr was also very visible in the 1990s, touring annually with his All-Star Band, a rotating group of rock veterans playing their hits on the summertime concert circuit. Beginning in 1988, Harrison recorded with Dylan, Tom Petty, Jeff Lynne, and Roy Orbison in a loose amalgam known as the Traveling Wilburys, but, for most of the 1980s and '90s, he had a low profile as a musician while acting as the producer of several successful films. After surviving a knife attack at his home in 1999, Harrison succumbed to a protracted battle with cancer in 2001.

Early in the 1990s McCartney, Harrison, and Starr had joined to add harmonies to two previously unreleased vocal recordings by Lennon. These new songs by "the Beatles" served as a pretext for yet another publicity blitz, aimed at creating a market for a lavishly produced quasi-historical series of archival recordings assembled under the supervision of the band and released in 1995 and 1996 as *The Beatles Anthology*, a collection of six compact discs that supplemented a 10-hour-long authorized video documentary of the same name. A compilation of the band's number one singles, *1*, appeared in 2000 and enjoyed worldwide success, topping the charts in such countries as England and the United States.

The Beatles were inducted into the Rock and Roll Hall of Fame in 1988, and Lennon (1994), McCartney (1999), and Harrison (2004) were also inducted as solo performers. In April 2009 it was announced that on September 9 there would be a simultaneous release of specially packaged, digitally remastered versions of the Beatles' entire catalog and a Beatles version of the popular electronic music game *Rock Band*.

JOAN BAEZ
(b. Jan. 9, 1941, Staten Island, N.Y., U.S.)

American folksinger and political activist Joan Chandos Baez interested young audiences in folk music during the 1960s. Despite the inevitable fading of the folk music revival, Baez continued to be a popular performer into the 21st century. By touring with younger performers throughout the world and staying politically engaged, she reached a new audience both in the United States and abroad.

The daughter of a physicist of Mexican descent whose teaching and research took him to various communities in New York, California, and elsewhere, Baez moved often and acquired little formal musical training. Her first instrument was the ukulele, but she soon learned to accompany her clear soprano voice on the guitar. Her first album, *Joan Baez*, was released in 1960. Although some considered her voice too pretty, her youthful attractiveness and activist energy put her in the forefront of the 1960s folk-song revival, popularizing traditional songs through her performances in coffeehouses, at music festivals, and on television and through her record albums, which were best sellers from 1960 through 1964 and remained popular. She was instrumental in the early career of Bob Dylan, with whom she was romantically involved for several years. Two of the songs with which she is most

This photo, taken at a Washington, D.C., civil rights rally in 1963, shows folk singers Joan Baez and Bob Dylan performing.

identified are her 1971 cover of the Band's song "The Night They Drove Old Dixie Down" and her own song "Diamonds and Rust," which she recorded on her acclaimed album of the same name, issued in 1975.

An active participant in the 1960s protest movement, Baez made free concert appearances for UNESCO, civil rights organizations, and anti-Vietnam War rallies. In 1964 she refused to pay federal taxes that went toward war expenses, and she was jailed twice in 1967. Throughout the years, she remained deeply committed to social and political causes, lending her voice in many concerts for a variety of causes. Among Baez's noteworthy recordings are *Diamonds and Rust*, *Very Early Joan* (1983), *Speaking of Dreams* (1989), *Play Me Backwards* (1992), *Gone from Danger* (1997), and *Bowery Songs* (2004). She wrote *Daybreak* (1968), an auto-biography, and a memoir titled *And a Voice to Sing With* (1987).

PLÁCIDO DOMINGO
(b. Jan. 21, 1941, Madrid, Spain)

Spanish-born singer, conductor, and opera administrator Plácido Domingo, with his resonant, powerful voice, imposing physical stature, good looks, and remarkable dramatic ability, was one of the most popular tenors of his time.

Domingo's parents were noted performers in zarzuela, a form of Spanish light opera. The family moved to Mexico when he was eight. He studied piano and conducting at the National Conservatory of Music, but he changed his emphasis when his rich vocal ability was revealed. In 1961 he made his operatic debut in Mexico City and then went to Dallas to perform in its opera company. From 1962 to 1965 he was a resident performer at Tel Aviv's Hebrew

National Opera. He made his debut at the New York City Opera in 1965, at the Metropolitan Opera House in New York City in 1968 (subsequently becoming a regular performer there), and at La Scala in Milan in 1969. Over the course of an opera career that lasted more than 45 years, Domingo sang an unprecedented number of different roles—more than 120—and he continued to learn new parts into his 60s.

A prolific and versatile performer, Domingo made numerous recordings and several film versions of operas, and he ventured into popular music as well. With Luciano Pavarotti and José Carreras, he performed around the world as one of the "Three Tenors," exposing millions of people to the operatic repertoire. He received 11 Grammy Awards in several categories, as well as a Kennedy Center Honor (2000), the U.S. Medal of Freedom (2002), and an honorary British knighthood (2002), among many other honours. In 2009 he was awarded the first Birgit Nilsson Prize for outstanding achievement in classical music.

From 1996 he was artistic director, then from 2001 general director, of the Washington (D.C.) Opera, and from 2000 he was general director of the Los Angeles Opera. Domingo also conducted major symphony and opera orchestras in the United States and Europe. His motto, he claimed, was "If I rest, I rust." His autobiography, *My First Forty Years*, was published in 1983.

THE BEACH BOYS

The original members were Brian Wilson (b. June 20, 1942, Inglewood, Calif., U.S.), Dennis Wilson (b. Dec. 4, 1944, Inglewood, Calif., U.S.—d. Dec. 28, 1983, Marina del Rey, Calif.), Carl Wilson (b. Dec. 21, 1946, Los Angeles, Calif., U.S.—d. Feb. 6, 1998, Los Angeles), Michael Love (b. March 15, 1941, Los Angeles, Calif., U.S.), and Alan

Jardine (b. Sept. 3, 1942, Lima, Ohio, U.S.). Significant later members included David Marks (b. Aug. 22, 1948, Newcastle, Pa., U.S.) and Bruce Johnston (original name William Baldwin; b. June 24, 1944, Chicago, Ill., U.S.)

The dulcet melodies and distinctive vocal mesh of the American rock group the Beach Boys defined the 1960s youthful idyll of sun-drenched southern California.

Initially perceived as a potent pop act—celebrants of the surfing and hot rod culture of the Los Angeles Basin during the 1960s—the Beach Boys and lead singer-bassist-producer Brian Wilson later gained greater respect as muses of post-World War II American suburban angst. Notwithstanding sales of 70 million albums, their greatest achievement was their ability to express the bittersweet middle-class aspirations of those who had participated in America's great internal westward movement in the 1920s. The Beach Boys extolled the promise of a fragile California dream that their parents had had to struggle to sustain.

Growing up in suburban Los Angeles (Hawthorne), the Wilson brothers were encouraged by their parents to explore music. Their father, Murry, who operated a small machinery shop, was also a songwriter. While still teenagers, Brian, drummer Dennis, and guitarist Carl joined with cousin Love and friends Jardine and Marks to write and perform pop music in the alloyed spirit of Chuck Berry and the harmonies-driven Four Freshmen and Four Preps.

Dennis, a novice surfer and adolescent habitué of the Manhattan Beach surfing scene, goaded Brian and the rest of the group (then called the Pendletons) into writing songs that glorified the emerging sport. The regional success in 1961 of the Beach Boys' first single, "Surfin'," led in 1962 to their signing as Capitol Records' first rock act. Brian's latent ambitions as a pop composer were unleashed;

for years he would write almost all the group's songs, often with collaborators (most frequently Love). The Beach Boys soon appeared on *Billboard*'s U.S. singles charts with such odes to cars and surfing as "409" and "Surfin' Safari," while their debut album reached number 14. After the commercial triumph of the follow-up album and single, "Surfin' U.S.A.," in 1963, Brian assumed complete artistic control. Their next album, *Surfer Girl*, was a landmark for the unheard-of studio autonomy he secured from Capitol as writer, arranger, and producer. Redolent of the Four Freshmen but actually inspired by "When You Wish Upon a Star" from Walt Disney's film *Pinocchio* (1940), the title track combined a childlike yearning with sophisticated pop poignance. Like his hero, pioneering producer Phil Spector, the eccentric Brian proved gifted at crafting eclectic arrangements with crisply evocative rock power (e.g., "Little Deuce Coupe," "Fun, Fun, Fun," "I Get Around," and "Don't Worry Baby").

After the first of a series of stress- and drug-related breakdowns in 1964, Brian withdrew from touring and was replaced first by singer-guitarist Glen Campbell, then by veteran surf singer-musician Johnston. Brian focused thereafter on the Beach Boys' studio output, surpassing all his role models with his band's masterwork, *Pet Sounds* (1966). A bittersweet pastiche of songs recalling the pangs of unrequited love and other coming-of-age trials, *Pet Sounds* was acknowledged by Paul McCartney as the catalyst for the Beatles' *Sgt. Pepper's Lonely Hearts Club Band* (1967). Brian soon eclipsed himself again with "Good Vibrations," a startlingly prismatic "pocket symphony" that reached number one in the autumn of 1966. His self-confidence stalled, however, when an even more ambitious project called *Dumb Angel*, then *Smile*, failed to meet its appointed completion date in December 1966. Exhausted and depressed, Brian went into seclusion as the rest of the band cobbled remains of the abortive album into a tuneful but tentative release titled *Smiley Smile* (1967).

For the remainder of the decade, the Beach Boys issued records of increasing commercial and musical inconsistency. They departed Capitol amid a legal battle over back royalties and signed with Warner Brothers in 1970. When the splendid *Sunflower* sold poorly, Brian became a recluse, experimenting with hallucinogens and toiling fitfully while the rest of the group produced several strong but modest-selling albums in the early 1970s. Meanwhile, *Endless Summer*, a greatest hits compilation, reached number one in the charts in 1974. In 1976 an uneven but commercially successful album, *15 Big Ones*, signaled the reemergence of the still drug-plagued Brian. In 1977 Dennis released a critically acclaimed solo album, *Pacific Ocean Blue*. Despite personal turmoil, the reunited Beach Boys seemed destined for a new artistic peak when Dennis drowned in 1983. The excellent *The Beach Boys* was released in 1985. In 1988 Brian released a critically acclaimed self-titled solo album, the other Beach Boys had a number one hit with "Kokomo," and the group was inducted into the Rock and Roll Hall of Fame. In the 1990s the Beach Boys continued to tour and record, with Love continuing his longtime role as the band's business mind. Brian released another solo album (*Imagination*) and collaborated on albums with Van Dyke Parks (*Orange Crate Art*) and with his daughters Carnie and Wendy (*The Wilsons*), who were successful performers in their own right. Carl, who was considered the group's artistic anchor during the turbulent 1970s and '80s, died of cancer in 1998.

In 2004 Brian released *Gettin' In over My Head*, with contributions from Paul McCartney, Eric Clapton, and Elton John. The landmark work of this period in Brian's career, however, was his solo album, *Smile*. He was presented with a Kennedy Center Honor in 2007, and in 2008 he released *That Lucky Old Sun*, a nostalgic celebration of southern California made in collaboration with Scott Bennett and Parks.

BOB DYLAN
(b. May 24, 1941, Duluth, Minn., U.S.)

American folksinger Bob Dylan (born Robert Allen Zimmerman) moved from folk to rock music in the 1960s and infused the lyrics of rock and roll, theretofore concerned mostly with boy-girl romantic innuendo, with the intellectualism of classic literature and poetry. Dylan has sold more than 58 million albums, written more than 500 songs recorded by more than 2,000 artists, and performed all over the world.

He grew up in the northeastern Minnesota mining town of Hibbing, where his father co-owned Zimmerman Furniture and Appliance Co. He acquired his first guitar at age 14 and as a high school student played in a series of rock and roll bands. In 1959, just before enrolling at the University of Minnesota in Minneapolis, he served a brief stint playing piano for rising pop star Bobby Vee. Fascinated by folksinger Woody Guthrie, he began performing folk music in coffeehouses, adopting the last name Dylan (after the Welsh poet Dylan Thomas). Restless and determined to meet Guthrie—who was confined to a hospital in New Jersey—he relocated to the East Coast.

Arriving in late January 1961, Dylan relied on the generosity of various benefactors who, charmed by his performances in Greenwich Village, provided meals and shelter. He quickly built a following and within four months was hired to play harmonica for a Harry Belafonte recording session. In September 1961 talent scout–producer John Hammond, Sr., signed him to Columbia Records.

Dylan's eponymous first album was released in March 1962 to mixed reviews. His singing voice—a cowboy lament laced with Midwestern patois, with an obvious nod to Guthrie—confounded many critics. By comparison, Dylan's second album, *The Freewheelin' Bob Dylan* (released in May 1963), sounded a clarion call. Young ears everywhere quickly assimilated his quirky voice, which established him as part of the burgeoning counterculture. Moreover, his first major composition, "Blowin' in the Wind," served notice that this was no cookie-cutter recording artist. About this time Dylan signed a seven-year management contract with Albert Grossman, who soon replaced Hammond with another Columbia producer, Tom Wilson.

In April 1963 Dylan played his first major New York City concert at Town Hall. That summer, Dylan made his first appearance at the Newport (Rhode Island) Folk Festival and was virtually crowned the king of folk music. The prophetic title song of his next album, *The Times They Are A-Changin'* (1964), provided an instant anthem.

Dylan was perceived as a singer of protest songs, a politically charged artist with a whole other agenda. He spawned imitators at coffeehouses and record labels everywhere. At the 1964 Newport Folk Festival, while previewing songs from *Another Side of Bob Dylan*, he confounded his core audience by performing songs of a personal nature, rather than his signature protest repertoire. A backlash from purist folk fans began and continued for three years as Dylan defied convention at every turn.

On his next album, *Bringing It All Back Home* (1965), electric instruments were openly brandished—a violation of folk dogma—and only two protest songs were included. The folk rock group the Byrds covered "Mr. Tambourine Man" from that album, adding electric 12-string guitar and three-part harmony vocals, and took it to number one on the singles chart. Dylan's mainstream audience skyrocketed. His purist folk fans, however, fell off in droves.

In June 1965 Dylan recorded his most ascendant song yet, "Like a Rolling Stone." Devoid of obvious protest references, set against a rough-hewn, twangy rock underpinning, and fronted by a snarling vocal that lashed out at all those who questioned his legitimacy, "Like a Rolling Stone" spoke to yet a new set of listeners and reached number two on the popular music charts. And the album containing the hit single, *Highway 61 Revisited*, further vindicated his abdication of the protest throne.

At the 1965 Newport Folk Festival, Dylan bravely showcased his electric sound. After an inappropriately short 15-minute set, Dylan left the stage to a hail of booing—mostly a response to the headliner's unexpectedly abbreviated performance rather than to his electrification. Nonetheless, reams were written about his electric betrayal and banishment from the folk circle. By the time of his next public appearance, at the Forest Hills (New York) Tennis Stadium a month later, the audience had been "instructed" by the press how to react. After a well-received acoustic opening set, Dylan was joined by his new backing band (Al Kooper on keyboards, Harvey Brooks on bass, and, from the Hawks, Canadian guitarist Robbie Robertson and drummer Levon Helm). Dylan and the band were booed throughout the performance.

Backed by Robertson, Helm, and the rest of the Hawks (Rick Danko on bass, Richard Manuel on piano, and Garth Hudson on organ and saxophone), Dylan toured incessantly in 1965 and 1966, always playing to sold-out audiences. On Nov. 22, 1965, Dylan married Sara Lowndes.

They split their time between a townhouse in Greenwich Village and a country estate in Woodstock, New York.

In February 1966, at the suggestion of his new producer, Bob Johnston, Dylan recorded at Columbia's Nashville, Tennessee, studios, along with Kooper, Robertson, and the cream of Nashville's studio musicians. A week's worth of marathon sessions produced *Blonde on Blonde*. The critically acclaimed album pushed Dylan to the zenith of his popularity. He toured Europe with the Hawks (soon to reemerge as the Band) until the summer of 1966, when a motorcycle accident in Woodstock brought Dylan's amazing seven-year momentum to an abrupt halt. He retreated to his home in Woodstock and virtually disappeared for two years.

In 1967 the Band moved to Woodstock to be closer to Dylan. Occasionally they coaxed him into the basement studio of their communal home to play music together, and recordings from these sessions ultimately became the double album *The Basement Tapes* (1975). In early 1968 Columbia released a stripped-down album of new Dylan songs titled *John Wesley Harding*. It reached number two on the pop album charts.

In January 1968 Dylan made his first postaccident appearance at a memorial concert for Woody Guthrie in New York City—with shorter hair, spectacles, and a neglected beard. At this point Dylan adopted the stance he held for the rest of his career: sidestepping the desires of the critics, he went in any direction but those called for in print. When his audience and critics were convinced that his muse had left him, Dylan would deliver an album at full strength, only to withdraw again.

Dylan returned to Tennessee to record *Nashville Skyline* (1969), which helped launch an entirely new genre, country rock. It charted at number three, but, owing to the comparative simplicity of its lyrics, people questioned whether

Dylan remained a cutting-edge artist. Meanwhile, rock's first bootleg album, *The Great White Wonder*—containing unreleased, "liberated" Dylan recordings—appeared in independent record stores.

Over the next quarter century Dylan continued to record, toured sporadically, and was widely honoured, though his impact was never as great or as immediate as it had been in the 1960s. In 1970 Princeton University awarded him an honorary doctorate of music. In August 1971 Dylan made a rare appearance at a benefit concert that former Beatle George Harrison had organized for the newly independent country of Bangladesh. At the end of the year, Dylan purchased a house in Malibu, California; he had already left Woodstock for New York City in 1969.

In 1973 he appeared in director Sam Peckinpah's film *Pat Garrett and Billy the Kid* and contributed to the soundtrack, including "Knockin' on Heaven's Door." *Writings and Drawings*, an anthology of his lyrics and poetry, was published the next year. In 1974 he toured for the first time in eight years, reconvening with the Band.

Released in January 1975, Dylan's next studio album, *Blood on the Tracks*, was a return to lyrical form. It topped the charts, as did *Desire*, released one year later. In 1975 and 1976 Dylan toured North America, announcing shows only hours before appearing. Filmed and recorded, the *Rolling Thunder Revue*—including Joan Baez, Allen Ginsberg, Ramblin' Jack Elliott, and Roger McGuinn—came to motion-picture screens in 1978 as part of the Dylan-edited *Renaldo and Clara*.

Lowndes and Dylan divorced in 1977. They had four children, including son Jakob, whose band, the Wallflowers, experienced pop success in the 1990s. Dylan was also stepfather to a child from Lowndes's previous marriage. In 1978 Dylan mounted a yearlong world tour and released

Bob Dylan performed in Rotterdam, Netherlands, as part of his 1978 tour.

Street-Legal and *Bob Dylan at Budokan*. In a dramatic turnabout, he converted to Christianity in 1979 and for three years recorded and performed only religious material. He received a Grammy Award in 1980 for best male rock vocal performance with his "gospel" song "Gotta Serve Somebody."

By 1982, when Dylan was inducted into the Songwriters Hall of Fame, his open zeal for Christianity was waning. In 1985 he participated in the all-star charity recording "We Are the World," organized by Quincy Jones, and published his third book, *Lyrics: 1962–1985*. Dylan toured again in 1986–87, backed by Tom Petty and the Heartbreakers. A year later he was inducted into the Rock and Roll Hall of Fame, and the Traveling Wilburys (Dylan, Petty, Harrison, Jeff Lynne, and Roy Orbison) formed at his house in Malibu and released their first album. In 1989 Dylan once again returned to form with *Oh Mercy*.

When *Life* magazine published a list of the 100 most influential Americans of the 20th century in 1990, Dylan was included, and in 1991 he received a Grammy Award for lifetime achievement. As the 1990s drew to a close, Dylan, who was called the greatest poet of the second half of the 20th century by Allen Ginsberg, was the recipient of several national and international honours. In 1998, in a comeback of sorts, he won three Grammy Awards—including album of the year—for *Time Out of Mind*. Another Grammy (for best contemporary folk album) came Dylan's way in 2001, for *Love and Theft*.

In 2003 he cowrote and starred in the film *Masked & Anonymous* and, because of the effects of carpal tunnel syndrome, began playing electric piano exclusively in live appearances. The next year he released what portended to be the first in a series of autobiographies, *Chronicles: Volume 1*. In 2005 *No Direction Home*, a documentary directed by Martin Scorsese, appeared on television. In 2006 Dylan turned his attention to satellite radio as the host of the weekly *Theme Time Radio Hour* and released his 44th album, *Modern Times*, which won the 2007 Grammy Award for best contemporary folk album.

In presenting to Dylan Spain's Prince of Asturias Prize for the Arts in 2007, the jury called him a "living myth in the history of popular music and a light for a generation that dreamed of changing the world." In 2008 the Pulitzer Prize Board awarded him a special citation for his "profound impact on popular music and American culture." Dylan was still actively performing in his 80s.

Glossary

amalgam: A fusion of different elements.

anathema: A person or thing that is detested, especially by the church.

avant-garde: Experimental or progressive.

diatonic: A scale of the type represented by the white keys on a piano.

dulcet: Characterized by soothing, melodious tones.

ebullient: Overflowing with enthusiasm.

eponymous: Named after a particular person; self-titled.

glaucoma: An eye disease caused by increased pressure that damages the optic nerve.

oratorio: A musical composition for voices and orchestra that tells a sacred story without costumes, scenery, or dramatic action.

sycophant: A person looking for recognition by flattering the influential and powerful.

tonality: The emphasis of a single pitch (tonic) as the center of a composition.

vibrato: A rapid, repetitive fluctuation of pitch on a sustained vocal or instrumental tone.

For More Information

BOOKS

Heylin, Clinton. *The Double Life of Bob Dylan: A Restless, Hungry Feeling, 1941–1966*. New York, NY: Little, Brown and Company, 2021.

Lopes, Paul Douglas. *Art Rebels: Race, Class, and Gender in the Art of Miles Davis and Martin Scorsese*. Princeton, N.J.: Princeton University Press, 2019.

Riding, Alan, Leslie Dunton-Downer. *Opera: The Definitive Illustrated Story*. New York, NY: DK, 2022.

Thomson, Elizabeth M. *Joan Baez: The Last Leaf*. London, England: Palazzo Editions Ltd, 2020.

WEBSITES

The Beatles
www.thebeatles.com
Visit this website to read news about the surviving members of The Beatles and performances of the band's music.

Recording Academy Grammy Awards
www.grammy.com
Keep up to date on nominees and winners of the Grammy Awards.

Rock and Roll Hall of Fame
www.rockhall.com
Learn about all the musical acts that have been inducted into the Rock and Roll Hall of Fame over the years.

Index

Baez, Joan, 47–49, 58
Beach Boys, 11, 50–54
Beatles, 11, 25, 30–32, 34, 41–47, 52, 58
Berry, Chuck, 9–12, 45, 51
blues, 8, 10–11, 14, 20–21, 30–32, 34
bossa nova, 12–13
Brown, James, 18–20

Charles, Ray, 14–16
classical music, 12–13, 37
Cline, Patsy, 16–18
country, 10–11, 16–17, 20–22, 28, 34, 57

Davis, Miles, 6–9, 35
Domingo, Plácido, 49–50
Dylan, Bob, 24–25, 30, 37, 45, 46, 48, 54–61

folk, 42, 44, 47–48, 54–56

Glass, Philip, 36–37
gospel, 14, 16, 18, 20–21, 28, 60
Grammy Awards, 9, 12, 15–16, 27, 30, 50, 60–61

Holly, Buddy, 28–30, 45

jazz, 6–9, 13–14, 16, 20, 38
Jobim, Antonio Carlos "Tom," 12–14

Kennedy Center Honor, 16, 27, 50, 54

Motown, 37–38

opera, 26–37, 36–37, 49–50

Pavarotti, Luciano, 26–27, 50
pop music, 10–13, 16–18, 20–21, 27, 38, 44, 46, 50–52, 54, 57–58
Presley, Elvis, 21–26, 28, 45

rhythm and blues, 10–11, 14, 16, 18, 25, 28, 38, 40
rock, 9–12, 17–18, 22, 24–25, 28–33, 36, 42, 44–45, 51–52, 54, 56–58
rockabilly, 21, 24
Rock and Roll Hall of Fame, 12, 16, 20, 30, 39, 47, 53, 60
Rolling Stones, 11, 25, 30–36

samba, 12–13
Smokey Robinson and the Miracles, 37–39
soul, 14, 18–19, 39